-63-
Comical Songs
for the
Ukulele
Fun For All Ages!
Arranged by Dick Sheridan

To access audio visit:
www.halleonard.com/mylibrary

Enter Code
1646-0217-0865-7119

Audio tracks are provided so melodies and chord progressions can be heard, and to allow the reader to play along with songs. The tracks are digitally generated and are not from a live recording.

ISBN 978-1-57424-366-6
SAN 683-8022

Cover by James Creative Group

Cover Photo of the "Harold Teen" Ukulele by Sandor Nagyszalanczxy

Copyright © 2018 CENTERSTREAM Publishing
P.O. Box 17878 - Anaheim Hills, CA 92817

www.centerstream-usa.com | centerstrm@aol.com | 714-779-9390

All rights for publication and distribution are reserved.
No part of this book may be reproduced in any form or by any Electronic or mechanical means including information storage and retrieval systems without permission in writing from the publisher, except by reviewers who may quote brief passages in review.

Contents

ABOUT THE ARRANGER

Dick Sheridan likes to think of himself as the Good Humor Man of the ukulele, not in the sense of ice cream trucks blaring musical jingles and ringing bells but in the enjoyment of singing and playing songs filled with fun and laughter. Like most of us, his appreciation of life's funny side began in childhood. He remembers lying on the living room floor reading the Sunday funnies, then graduating to comic and joke books, later enhanced with the wonderful world of humorous movies, Saturday morning TV cartoons, and the side-splitting insanity of radio and sitcom television shows.

Then came the discovery of funny songs. It was a natural evolution that blended an appreciation for the absurd and his ability early on to play the ukulele. He started by serenading baby sitting charges with limericks often set to his own music. Kids love comic songs, the rhymes, the rhythms, the unexpected,. And Dick does too. He gleaned whatever funny songs he could find from friends, family music books, and novelty phonograph recordings. Eventually he moved from baby sitting to college dorm sessions, summer camping, beach parties, and sing-along gatherings with audiences just as enthusiastic as he for the sheer pleasure of nonsense and the twists and turns of convoluted logic.

Dick's sense of fun came from a good-natured mother who always enjoyed a joke, a bit of silliness, even wearing a Halloween mask when it wasn't Halloween, and catching you offguard with a surprise BOO! His father's wit and dry sense of humor led to many a laughable encounter, like when he'd catch his dad heading for the bathroom shower with his raincoat on, wearing galoshes, and carrying an umbrella.

Dick has found that silly songs are always popular and often the ones most called for. Accompanying them on the ukulele is much easier (and less cumbersome) than with other instruments and a lot more fun that singing a capella.

The field of silly music is rich and ever changing. New songs constantly emerge and old favorites are always at the ready. Some songs are laid back, gentle, and with mild humor. Others are wild, inane, and right off the wall. Whichever, Dick says you don't have to be a ukulele virtuoso to play them. Just a few basic chords and you're on your way. Start easy with songs that require only two or three chords. Play the tablature until the melody is fixed in your mind and under your finger tips, then get your voice in the right pitch. If you can read standard notation, all the better. It will help you with the timing, but of course so will the online audio.

Just like in the song "Groundhog" (included in this collection) where Sally steps up with a "snigger and a grin," you'll be doing the same in the zany musical world of unbridled insanity and merriment. See for yourself how contagious the laughter is when you hold forth with songs like "A Capital Ship," "Peeping Thru the Knothole of Grandpa's Wooden Leg" or "Mrs. Murphy's Chowder."

There's lots more from this song-bag of Dick's favorites. It's time to be silly, put on a funny hat, glue a maple see helicopter to your nose, don a false mustache. Throw caution to the winds and walk on the wild side. To twist a phrase from an old jazz standard: "Grab your hat and get your coat, leave your worries on the doorstep, just direct your feet to the FUNNY side side of the street."

INTRODUCTION

"...What fools these mortals be!"
(Spoken by mischievous Puck in Shakespeare's "Midsummer's Night Dream")

We all enjoy a good laugh and there are loads of them in this collection of silly and comic songs. The pages are filled with musical jokes, songs that are preposterous, nonsensical, absurd, outlandish – but all are fun and guaranteed to bring a smile and a tickle to your funny bone.

Indeed, some of these songs stretch the imagination far beyond belief-- from the sublime to the ridiculous, as they say -- and we wouldn't have it any other way. Here are songs featuring impossible situations, crazy twists and turns, foolishness, and tongue-in-cheek spoofs designed to throw you off guard, trigger your sense of humor, and hoodwink your listeners.

Quite a few songs are "anthropomorphic" – that is, ascribing human characteristics to animals like singing frogs, misbehaving goats, and pigs that get measles. Many songs are loaded with "non sequiturs" – situations with illogical unexpected endings. Good examples are limericks, and you'll see how to set them to music in one of the following songs: "In China They Never Eat Chili."

It may surprise you that even a familiar song like "Yankee Doodle" contains unsuspected humor. Parodies sneak in putting funny lyrics to familiar tunes like "Turkey in the Straw," "On Top of Old Smoky," and the Mexican favorite "Cielito Lindo."

With a few modifications, even nursery rhymes and folk songs can provide a good source of belly laughs. And of course there's the output of the Broadway stage, vaudeville, the British music hall, and comic operettas. (See Centerstream's *The Songs of Gilbert & Sullivan for Ukulele*.)

Good-natured "gospel" songs are fair game too for the musical humorist. Is nothing sacred, you ask? Fortunately, no – not when it comes to songs that spoof Noah's ark, Pharaoh's daughter, and Jonah in the whale.

Time was – back in the early days before radio, television, and movies – entertainment was often provided by a JESTER, someone engaged to provide fun and amusement for the court of a noble household. Among his tasks were magic, juggling, story telling, jokes, and of course comical songs. Sometimes referred to as a FOOL, the jester kept things lively with buffoonery, laughter and silly antics. His songs were carefully molded to lampoon and saturize, weaving the tunes with wit, humor, and tom-foolery.

The jester's tradition of amusing songs is well preserved in the following pages. But for those of us performing them, there's no need for a foolscap with bells, just a well-tuned ukulele and a copy of this book with dozens and dozens of songs to choose from.

Whether these songs are unfamiliar or old standbys, you'll have plenty of fun exploring the following pages and finding songs that particularly tweak your sense of fun.

So then, with a wink and a nudge, and a gasping cry of "pull the other one," away we go on a whimsical silly adventure. Put your seat belt on and be prepared for a truly bizarre trip. It's time to break out your ukulele and get ready for loads of goofy good times along the way. All kidding aside, this is one book that's both fun and funny, one you're sure to return to over and over again.   Let's let our guiding motto be : Live, love, LAUGH and be happy!

~*~

THE ABA DABA HONEYMOON

Ukulele tuning: gCEA

ARTHUR FIELDS   WALTER DONOVAN

ABDULLAH BULBUL AMIR

Ukulele tuning: gCEA

Traditional

The sons of the des - ert are brave men and bold, and quite un - ac - cus - tomed to fear,_____ but the brav - est of all was a man, I am told, named Ab - dul - lah Bul - bul A - mir._____

ABDULLAH BULBUL AMIR

These lyrics are an extraction from much longer ones that can be found on the Internet.

This son of the desert in battle aroused,
Could split twenty men on his spear.
A terrible creature when sober or soused
Was Abdullah Bulbul Amir.

Now the heroes were plenty and well known to fame
Who fought in the ranks of the Czar,
But the bravest of these was a man by the name
Of Ivan Skavinsky Skivar.

He could dance the fandango, play poker or pool,
And strum on the Spanish guitar;
In fact, quite the cream of the Muscovite team
Was Ivan Skavinsky Skivar.

One day this bold Russian had shouldered his gun,
And donned his most truculent sneer,
Downtown he did go where he trod on the toe
Of Abdullah Bulbul Amir.

"Young man," quoth Abdullah, "has life grown so dull
That you're anxious to end your career?
Do you not know you have trod on the toe
Of Abullah Bulbul Amir?"

"So take your last look at the sunshine and brook,
And send your regrets to the Czar,
For by this I imply, you are going to die,
Mr. Ivan Skavinsky Skivar."

Said Ivan, "My friend, your remarks in the end
Will avail you but little, I fear;
For you ne'er will survive to repeat them alive,
Mr. Abdullah Bulbul Amir."

They parried and thrust, they sidestepped and cussed,
Of blood they spilled a great part;
The philologist blokes, who seldom crack jokes,
Said that hash was first made on that spot.

There's a tomb rises up where the Blue Danube rolls,
And graved there in characters clear
Are "Strangers, when passing, oh pray for the soul
Of Abdullah Bulbul Amir."

A CAPITAL SHIP

Ukulele tuning: gCEA

From a poem by:
CHARLES E. CARRYL

Traditional

D   A7   D

♩=140

1. A cap-it-al ship for an o-cean trip was the "Wal-lop-ing Win-dow Blind." No

E7   A   E7   A

wind that blew dis-mayed her crew or troubl-ed the cap-tain's mind. The

D   A7

man at the wheel was made to feel con-tempt for the wild-est blow,_____ tho' it

D   A7   D

oft ap-peared when the gale had cleared that he'd been in his bunk be-low. So,

A CAPITAL SHIP

2. The bo'sun's mate was very sedate, yet fond of amusements, too.
  He played hop-scotch with the starboard watch, while the captain tickled the crew.
  The gunner we had was apparently mad, for he sat on the after rai-ai-ail,
  And fired salutes with the captain's boots in the teeth of a booming gale.
  Chorus

3. The captain sat on the commodore's hat, and dined in a royal way
  Off pickles and figs, and little roast pigs, and gunnery bread each day.
  The cook was Dutch and behaved as such, for the diet he served the crew-ew-ew,
  Was a couple of tons of hot-cross buns served up with sugar and glue.
  Chorus

4. Then we all fell ill as mariners will on a diet that's rough and crude,
  And we shivered and shook as we dipped the cook in a tub of his gluesome food.
  All nautical pride we cast aside, and we ran the vessel ashore-ore-ore
  On the Gulliby Isles, where the poopoo smiles, and the rubbily ubdugs roar.
  Chorus

5. Composed of sand was that favored land, and trimmed with cinnamon straws,
  And pink and blue was the pleasing hue of the tickle-toe-teaser's claws.
  We sat on the edge of a sandy ledge, and shot at the whistling bee-ee-ee,
  While the ring-tailed bats wore waterproof hats as they dipped in the shining sea.
  Chorus

6. On rugbug bark from dawn till dark we dined till we all had grown
  Uncommonly shrunk, when a Chinese junk came up from the Torrible Zone.
  She was chubby and square, but we didn't much care, so we cheerily put to sea-ee-ee,
  And we left all the crew of the junk to chew on the bark of the rugbug tree.
  Chorus

BE KIND TO YOUR WEB FOOTED FRIENDS

(Melody: "Stars and Stripes Forever" by John Philip Sousa)

Ukulele tuning: gCEA

Words: Author Unknown

ALL FOR ME GROG

Ukulele tuning: gCEA

Traditional Sailor's Song

With an easy swing

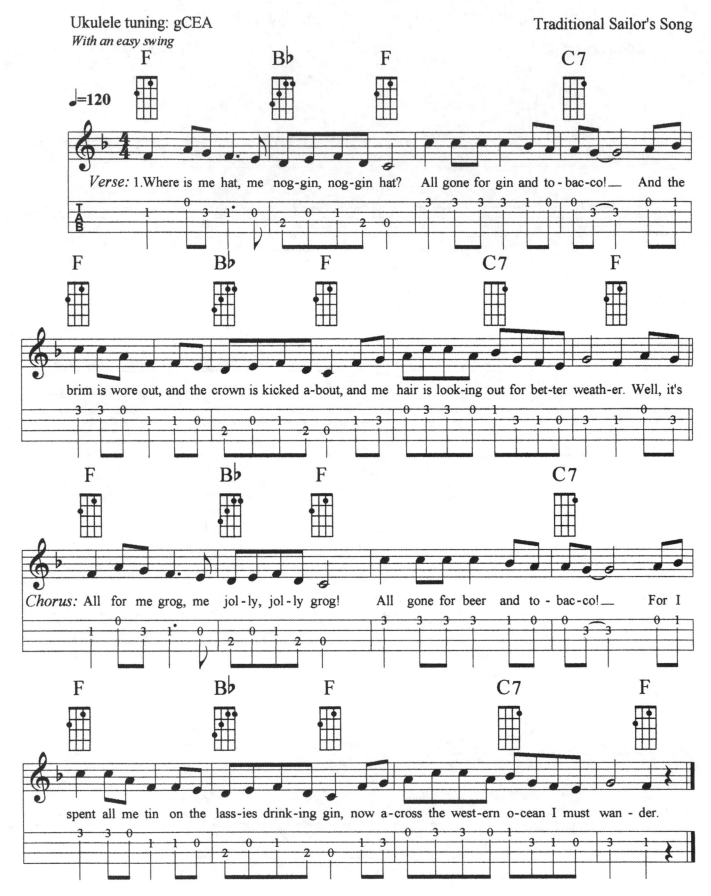

Verse: 1.Where is me hat, me nog-gin, nog-gin hat? All gone for gin and to-bac-co!__ And the

brim is wore out, and the crown is kicked a-bout, and me hair is look-ing out for bet-ter weath-er. Well, it's

Chorus: All for me grog, me jol-ly, jol-ly grog! All gone for beer and to-bac-co!__ For I

spent all me tin on the lass-ies drink-ing gin, now a-cross the west-ern o-cean I must wan - der.

2. Where is me shirt, me noggin, noggin shirt?
   All gone for gin and tobacco!
   And the sleeves are worn out,
   And the collar's knocked about,
   And the tails is looking out for better weather.
   Chorus

3. Where are me boots, me noggin, noggin boots?
   All gone for gin and tobacco!
   And the soles are worn out,
   And the heels are kicked about,
   And me toes are looking out for better weather.
   Chorus

4. Where are me pants, me noggin, noggin pants?
   All gone for gin and tobacco!
   And the cuffs are worn out,
   And the fly is knocked about,
   And me arse is looking out for better weather.
   Chorus

5. I'm sick to my head, and I haven't been to bed,
   Since I first came ashore with all me plunder;
   I see centipedes and snakes,
   And I'm full of pains and aches,
   And I guess it's time to shove off over yonder.
   Chorus

THE ANIMAL FAIR

Ukulele tuning: gCEA

Traditional

I   went to the An - i - mal Fair,   the   an - i - mals all   were there,   the

old   rac-coon by the light of the moon   was comb-ing his au - burn hair.   The

mon - key he   got queer,   he   climbed up   the   el - e - phant's ear.   The

el - e - phant sneezed   and fell on his knees   and that was the end of the monk,   the monk,   the

monk, the monk, the monk, the monk, and that was the end of the monk.

BILL GROGAN'S GOAT

Ukulele tuning: gCEA

Traditional

Verse 1: There was a man, now please take note, there was a man who had a goat. He loved that goat, in-deed he did, he loved that goat just like a kid.

Verse 2: One day that goat
Was feeling fine
Ate three red shirts
Right off the line.
His master came,
Gave him a whack,
And tied him to
A railroad track.

Verse 3: The whistle blew,
The train was nigh,
The poor goat knew
That he might die.
He gave three shrieks
Of mortal pain,
Coughed up the shirts
And flagged the train.

COCAINE BILL AND MORPHINE SUE

Ukulele tuning: gCEA

Traditional

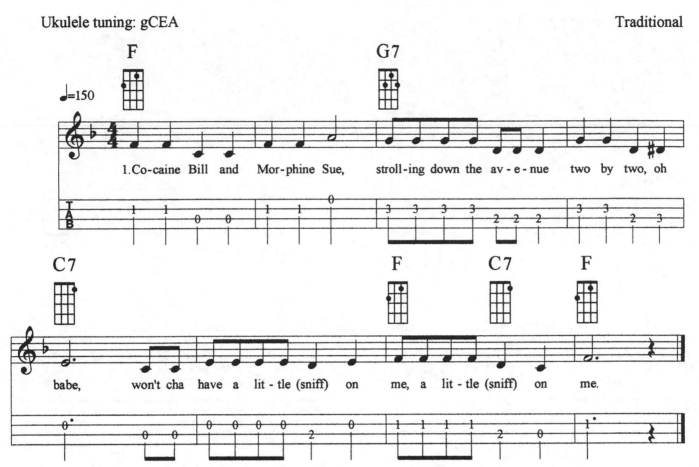

2. They walked up South and turned down Main,
   Lookin' for a place that sells cocaine,
   Oh, babe, won't cha have a little (sniff) on me,
   A little (sniff) on me.

3. Passed by a drug store full of smoke,
   Sign on the door said NO MORE COKE,
   Oh, babe, won't cha have a little (sniff) on me,
   A little (sniff) on me.

4. Said Sue to Bill, "Won't do no harm
   If we both have a little shot in the arm,"
   Oh, babe, won't cha have a little (sniff) on me,
   A little (sniff) on me.

5. Said Bill to Sue, "I can't refuse
   'Cause there's no more kick in beer or booze,
   Oh, babe, won't cha have a little (sniff) on me,
   A little (sniff) on me.

6. In a little grave up on a hill,
   Lies the body of Cocaine Bill,
   Oh, babe, won't cha have a little (sniff) on me,
   A little (sniff) on me.

7. In a little grave right by his side,
   Lies the body of his cocaine bride,
   Oh, babe, won't cha have a little (sniff) on me,
   A little (sniff) on me.

8. Now all you cokies are a-gonna be dead
   If you don't stop (sniff)in' that stuff in your head,
   Oh, babe, won't cha have a little (sniff) on me,
   A little (sniff) on me.

Every time there's a (sniff) make a sniffing sound ...

BILLY BOY

Ukulele tuning: gCEA

Traditional

BILLY BOY

Did she bid you to come in,
Billy Boy, Billy Boy,
Did she bid you to come in,
Charming Billy?
Yes, she bade me to come in,
There's a dimple in her chin,
She's a young thing
And cannot leave her mother.

Can she bake a cherry pie,
Billy Boy, Billy Boy,
Can she bake a cherry pie,
Charming Billy?
She can bake a cherry pie
Quick's a cat can wink an eye,
She's a young thing
And cannot leave her mother.

Did she set for you a chair,
Billy Boy, Billy Boy,
Did she set for you a chair,
Charming Billy?
Yes, she set for me a chair,
She has ringlets in her hair,
She's a young thing
And cannot leave her mother.

How old is she,
Billy Boy, Billy Boy,
How old is she,
Charming Billy?
Three times six and four times seven,
Twenty-eight and eleven,
She's a young thing
And cannot leave her mother.

My father once told me that he had something of a compulsion about adding numbers. He took the Long Island Railroad to work in New York City, and as he passed the idle cars in the Woodside freight yard just before entering the East River tunnel, he'd add up the numbers displayed on each car he passed.

If you have the same compulsion or are just curious, let's calculate the age numbers of Billy Boy's "young thing." 3x6=18, 4x7=28, plus 28 and 11. That makes a total of 85. A "young thing," indeed! Billy must have had a penchant for older women.

THE BOLL WEEVIL

Ukulele tuning: gCEA

Traditional

1. Oh, the boll wee-vil am a lit-tle black bug, come from Mex-i-co, they say, come all the way to Tex-as just a-look-in' for a place to stay, just a look-in' for a home, just a look-in' for a home.

2. The next time I seen the boll weevil
   He wa sitting on the square,
   The next time I seen the boll weevil
   He had all his family there,
   Just a-lookin' for a home,
   Just a-lookin' for a home.

THE BOLL WEEVIL

3. The farmer took the boll weevil
   Put him in the red hot sand,
   Boll weevil said to the farmer,
   "I can take it like a man,
   This'll be my home,
   This'll be my home."

4. The farmer took the boll weevil
   Put him on a block of ice,
   Boll weevil says to the farmer,
   "This is mighty cool and nice,
   This'll be my home,
   This'll be my home."

5. The farmer took the boll weevil
   Put him in the fire,
   Boll weevil says to the farmer,
   "This is just what I desire,
   This'll be my home,
   This'll be my home."

6. Boll weevil said to the farmer,
   "You had better leave me alone,
   I ate up all your cotton
   Now I'll eat up all your corn,
   I'll have a home,
   I'll have a home."

7. The merchant got half the cotton,
   The boll weevil got the rest,
   Didn't leave the farmer's wife
   But one old cotton dress,
   And it's full of holes,
   And it's full of holes.

8. Farmer said to his wife,
   "Now what d'ya think of that?
   The boll weevil made a nest
   In my old Stetson hat,
   Now it's full of holes,
   Now it's full of holes."

8. If anyone should ask you
   Who it was who sang this song,
   Say an Oklahoma farmer
   With a pair of blue jeans on.
   Now he's lookin' for a home,
   Now he's lookin' for a home.

CAPE COD GIRLS

Ukulele tuning: gCEA

Traditional

Verse: 1.Cape Cod girls they have no combs, Heave a - way! Heave a - way! They

comb their hair with cod - fish bones, we are bound for Cal - i - for - nia.

Chorus: Heave a - way, my bur - ly, bur - ly boys, Heave a - way! Heave a - way!

Heave a - way and don't you make a noise, we are bound for Cal - i - for - nia.

CAPE COD GIRLS

2. Cape Cod girls are very fine girls,
   Heave away! Heave a-way!
   With codfish balls they comb their curls,
   We are bound for California.
   Chorus

3. Cape Cod boys they have no sleds,
   Heave a-way! Heave a-way!
   They slide down hills on codfish heads,
   We are bound for California.
   Chorus

4. Cape Cod cats they have no tails,
   Heave a-way! Heave a-way!
   They lost them all in nor'east gales,
   We are bound for Califnornia.
   Chorus

5. Cape Cod doctors have no pills,
   Heave away! Heave a-way!
   They give their patients codfish gills,
   We are bound for California.
   Chorus

CAPTAIN JINKS OF THE HORSE MARINES

Ukulele tuning: gCEA

Traditional

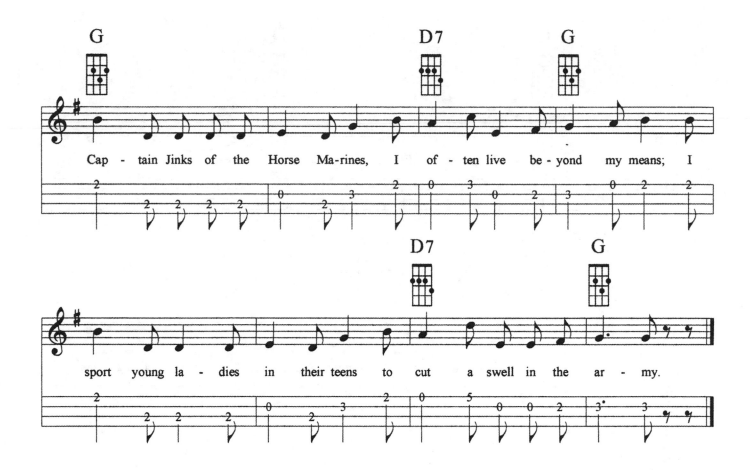

2. I'm Captain Jinks of the Horse Marines,
   I feed my horse good pork and beans;
   Of course 'tis quite beyond the means,
   Of a Captain in the army.
   I teach young ladies how to dance,
   How to dance, how to dance,
   I teach young ladies how to dance
   For I'm their pet in the army. Etc.

3. I joined the corps when twenty-one,
   Of course, I thought it capital fun,
   But when the enemy came I'd run,
   I wasn't cut out for the army.
   When I left home my Mama she cried,
   My Mama she cried, my Mama she cried,
   When I left home my Mama she cried,
   "He ain't cut out for ther army!" Etc.

THE RHYME OF THE CHIVALROUS SHARK

Ukulele tuning: gCEA

WALLACE IRWIN

THE RHYME OF THE CHIVALROUS SHARK

2. He dines upon seamen and skippers,
   And tourists his hunger assuage,
   And a fresh cabin boy
   Will inspire him with joy
   If he's past the maturity age.

3. A doctor, a lawyer, a preacher,
   He'll gobble one any fine day,
   But the ladies, God bless 'em,
   He'll only address 'em
   Politely and go on his way.

4. I can readily cite you an instance
   Where a lovely young lady of Breem,
   Who was tender and sweet
   And delicious to eat,
   Fell into the bay with a scream.

5. She struggled and flounced in the water,
   And signaled in vain for her bark,
   And she'd surely been drowned
   If she hadn't been found
   By a chivalrous man-eating shark.

6. He bowed in a manner most polished,
   Thus soothing her impulses wild.
   "Don't be frightened," he said,
   "I've been properly bread,
   And will eat neither woman nor child."

7. Then he proffered his fin and she took it,
   Such gallantry none can dispute,
   While the passengers cheered
   As the vessel they neared,
   And a broadside was fired in salute.

8. And they soon stood alongside the vessel,
   When a life-saving dinghy was lowered
   With the pick of the crew
   And her relatives too
   And the mate and the skipper aboard.

9. So they took her aboard in a jiffy,
   And the shark stood attention the while,
   Then he raised on his flipper
   And ate up the skipper
   And went on his way with a smile.

10. And this shows that the prince of the ocean
    To ladies forbearing and mild,
    Though his record be dark,
    Is the man-eating shark,
    Who will eat neither woman nor child.

THE DERBY RAM

Ukulele tuning: gCEA

With an easy swing.

Many versions of this British folk song exist with variations in both words and melodies. Derby (pronounced DAR-bee) is situated in Derbyshire county in the East Midlands of England.

Traditional

Verse 1. As I was goin' to Der - by up - on a mar - ket day, I saw the big - gest ram, sir, that ev - er was fed on hay.

2. The ram was fat behind, sir,
The ram was fat before.
He measured ten yards 'round, sir,
And maybe it was more.

3. He had four feet to walk upon,
He had four feet to stand.
And ev'ry foot that he set down
Covered an acre of ground.

4. The wool grew on his belly, sir,
It reached down to the ground.
'Twas sold in Derby Town, sir,
For forty thousand pounds.

5. The wool grew on his back, sir,
It reached up to the sky.
The eagles built their nests there,
I heard the young'uns cry.

6. The horns upon his head, sir,
Reached way up to the moon.
A boy climbed up in January
And didn't come down till June.

7. One of the ram's teeth, sir,
Was hollow as a horn.
When they took its measure, sir,
It held a bushel of corn.

8. The man that fed this ram, sir,
He fed him twice a day.
And when the ram was fed, sir,
He swallowed a bale of hay.

9. Indeed, sir, it's true, sir,
I've never been known to lie.
And had you been in Derby, sir,
You'd seen it same as I.

DO YOUR EARS HANG LOW?

Ukulele tuning: gCEA

Recognize this melody? Most of it is a quote from "Turkey in the Straw."

Traditional

2. Do your ears stick out?
   Can you wiggle 'em about?
   Can you flap 'em up and down
   As you fly around the town?
   Can you shut 'em up for sure
   If you hear and awful bore?
   Do your ears stick out?

3. Do your ears flip-flop?
   Can you use 'em as a mop?
   Are they stringy at the bottom?
   Are they curly at the top?
   Can you use 'em for a swatter?
   Can you use 'em for a blotter?
   Do your ears flip-flop?

THE DEVIL AND THE FARMER'S WIFE

Ukulele tuning: gCEA

Traditional

The Dev - il he came to a farm - er one day,

fol - di - rol - di, did - dle - i - day, the

Dev - il he came to a farm - er one day, said there's

"One in your fam - 'ly I"ll car - ry a - way," with a

THE DEVIL AND THE FARMER'S WIFE

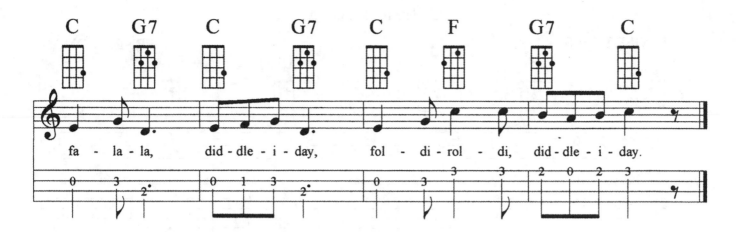

fa - la - la,   did - dle - i - day,   fol - di - rol - di,   did - dle - i - day.

"See here, my good man, I have come for your wife,"
Fol-di-rol-di, diddle-i-day,
"See here, my good man, I have come for your wife,
For she's a shrew and torment of your life,"
With a fa-la-la, diddle-i-day, fol-di-rol-di, diddle-i-day.

So the Devil he hoisted her up on his back,
Fol-di-rol-di, ETC.
So the Devil he hoisted her up on his back,
Down to hell he went, clickety-clack,
With a fa-la-la, ETC.

Ten little devils were playin' softball,
Fol-di-rol-di, ETC.
Ten little devils were playin' softball,
They said, "Take her away, she'll be the death of all,"
With a fa-la-la, ETC.

So the Devil he hoisted her up on his hump,
Fol-di-rol-di, ETC.
So the Devil he hoisted her up on his hump,
And back to earth with her he did jump,
With a fa-la-la, ETC.

"See here, my good man, I've come back with your wife,"
Fol-di-rol-di, ETC.
"See here, my good man, I've come back with your wife,
She's the bain and torment of my life,"
With a fa-la-la, ETC.

They say that the women are worse then the men,
Fol-di-rol-di, ETC.
They say that the women are worse then the men,
Got sent down to hell and got chucked up again,
With a fa-la-la, ETC.

DOWN IN THE U-17

Ukulele tuning: gCEA

ROGER LEWIS   ERNIE ERDMAN

The term U-boat comes from the German "unterseeboot" literally "under sea boat."

2. To all foreign ports went these jolly old sports
And torpedoed their way to the bar;
As their engines were cool they drank plenty of fuel.
They'd stay till the lights in the lighthouse went out,
Till they were all light in the head,
And hurry away to the boat in the bay
And sing as they jumped into bed.
Chorus

THE EDDYSTONE LIGHT

Ukulele tuning: gCEA

Traditional

1.My father was the keep-er of the Ed-dy-stone Light and he mar-ried a mer-maid one fine night. And from this un-ion there came three, a por-gy, and a por-poise, and the oth-er was me.

Yo, ho, ho, the wind blows free, oh, for a life on the roll-ing sea.

2. One fine night while a-trimmin' o' the glim
   And a-singing a verse from the evening hymn.
   A voice off starboard shouted, "Ahoy!"
   And there was my mother a-sitting on a buoy.
   Chorus

3. "What has become of my children three?"
   My mother then she asked of me.
   "One was exhibited as a talking fish
   And the other was served in a chafffing dish."
   Chorus

4. The phosphorus gleamed in her seaweed hair,
   I looked again and my mother wasn't there.
   A voice came echoing out of the night,
   "Your father was the keeper of the Eddystone Light.!"
   Chorus

NOTE: The Eddystone Light was a real lighthouse, located on the Eddystone Reef 14 miles from Plymouth off the storm-lashed coast of Cornwall. The dangerous reef was mostly submerged with only a small portion visible on which a succession of five lighthouses was built. After numerous ships floundered on the reef, the first Eddystone was erected in 1699, only to be destroyed four years later in one of the worst hurricanes ever recorded. It was rebuilt in 1803 and three times after that, the last constructed in 1882 -- a history spanning two centuries.

EGGS AND MARROWBONE

Ukulele tuning: gCEA

Traditional

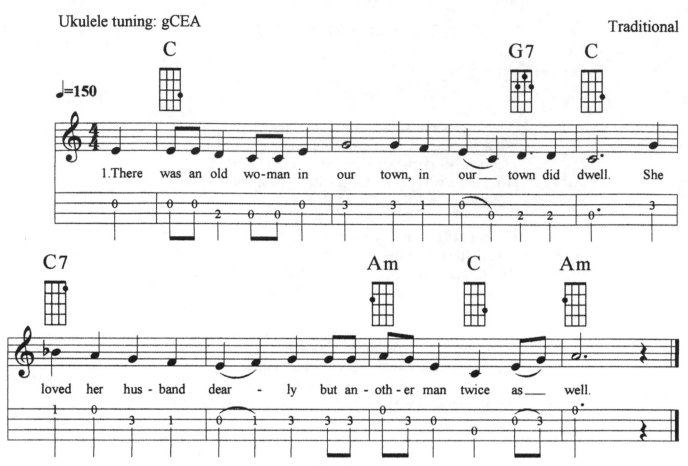

1. There was an old wo-man in our town, in our__ town did dwell. She loved her hus-band dear - ly but an-oth-er man twice as__ well.

2. She went to see the doctor
   To see what she could find.
   To see what she could find, sir,
   To make her old man blind.

3. Eggs, eggs, and marrowbone,
   Feed them to him all,
   That will make him so very blind
   That he can't see you at all.

4. She fed him eggs and marrowbone,
   Fed them to him all,
   That did make him so very blind
   That he couldn't see her at all.

5. Now that I am old and blind
   And tired of my life,
   I will go and drown myself
   And that will end my strife.

6. To drown yourself, to drown yourself,
   Now that would be a sin,
   So I'll go down to the water's edge
   And kindly push you in.

7. The old woman took a running jump
   For to push the old man in,
   The old man he stepped to one side
   And the old woman she fell in.

8. She called for help, she screamed for help,
   So loudly did she bawl.
   The old man said, "I'm so very blind
   That I can't see you at all."

9. She swam along, along swam she,
   Till she came to the river's edge,
   But the old man grabbed a big long pole
   And pushed her further in.

10. Now the old woman is dead and gone
    And the Devil's got her soul.
    Wasn't she a silly old fool
    Not to grab the old man's pole?

11. Eggs, eggs, and marrowbone
    Won't make your old man blind;
    If you really want to do him in
    Just sneak up from behind.

The theme of some nefarious plot at the river's edge is found elsewhere in traditional folk music, "The Banks of the Ohio" being one example. The intended victim usually sidesteps, the plot backfires, and the perpetrator becomes the victim.

THE E-RI-EE CANAL

2. Our captain he comes up on deck
   A spy glass in his hand,
   But the fog it was so 'tarnal thick
   That he couldn't spy the land. CHO.

3. Our cook she was a grand old gal,
   She had a ragged dress;
   We hoisted her up on a pole
   As a signal of distress. CHO.

4. We were loaded down with barley,
   We were chock up full of rye,
   The captain he looked down on me with a
   Goll darn wicked eye. CHO.

5. Two days our of Syracuse
   Our vessel struck a shoal,
   And we nearly foundered there on a
   Chunk of Lakawanna coal. CHO.

6. I hollered to the captain
   On the towpath treading dirt,
   He jumped on board and stopped a leak with his
   Old red flannel shirt. CHO.

7. Our captain he got married,
   Our cook she went to jail, and
   I'm the only sea cook's son who's
   Left to tell the tale. CHO.

FATHER'S WHISKERS

Ukulele tuning: gCEA

Traditional

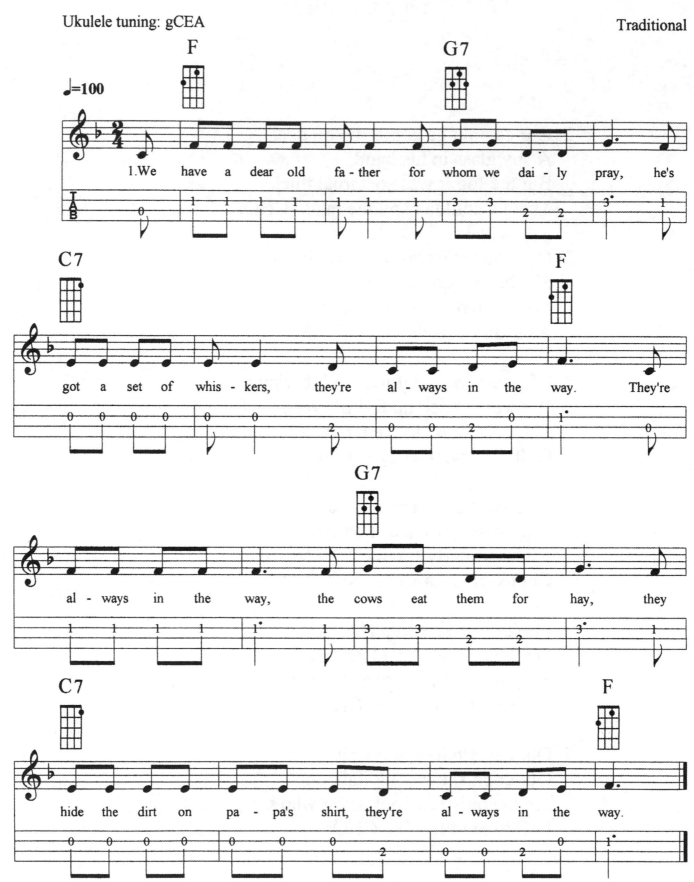

1.We have a dear old fa-ther for whom we dai-ly pray, he's got a set of whis-kers, they're al-ways in the way. They're al-ways in the way, the cows eat them for hay, they hide the dirt on pa-pa's shirt, they're al-ways in the way.

FATHER'S WHISKERS

Verse 2. When Father's in a tavern
He likes his lager beer,
He pins a pretzel to his nose
To keep his whiskers clear.
To keep his whiskers clear,
To keep his whiskers clear,
He pins a pretzel to his nose
To keep his whiskers clear.

Verse 3. Around the supper table,
We make a merry group,
Until dear Father's whiskers
Get tangled in the soup.
Get tangled in the soup,
Get tangled in the soup,
Until dear Father's whiskers
Get tangled in the soup.

Verse 4. When Father goes in swimming,
No bathing suit for him,
He ties his whiskers 'round his waist
And then he jumps right in.
And then he jumps right in,
And then he jumps right in,
He ties his whiskers 'round his waist
And then he jumps right in.

Verse 5. We have a dear old brother,
He's got a Ford machine,
He uses Father's whiskers
To strain the gasoline.
To strain the gasoline,
To strain the gasoline,
He uses Father's whiskers
To strain the gasoline.

FROGGIE WENT A-COURTING

Ukulele tuning: gCEA

Traditional

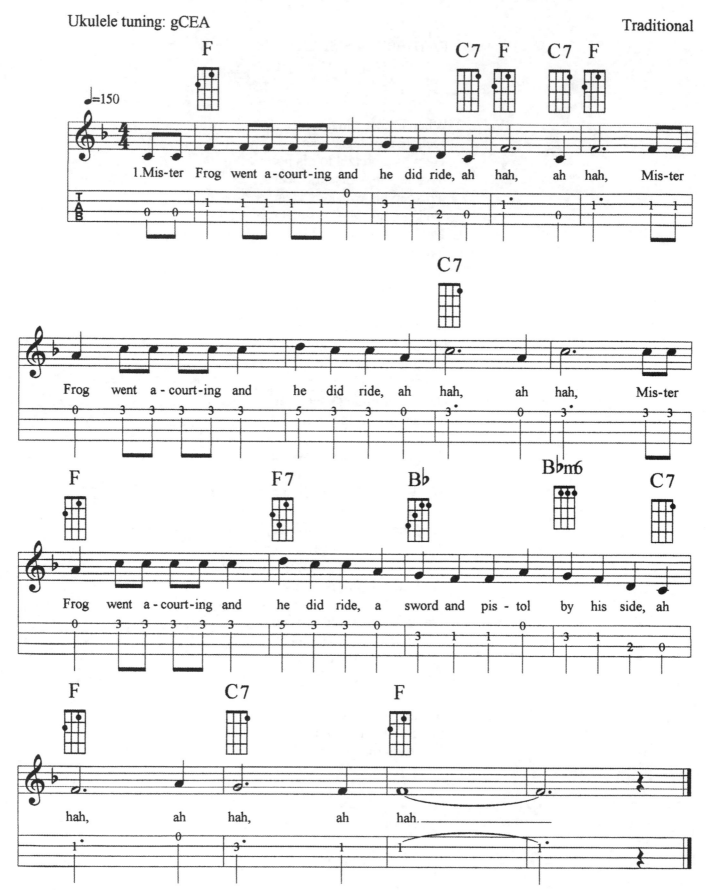

FROGGIE WENT A-COURTING

2. He rode up to Miss Mousie's door, ah hah, ah hah,
   He rode up to Miss Mousie's door, ah hah, ah hah,
   He rode up to Miss Mousie's door where he had been many times before,
   Ah hah, ah hah, ah hah.

3. He said, "Miss Mousie are you within?" ah hah, ah hah (2 times)
   She said, "Mr. Frog I sit and spin, just lift the latch and please come in."
   Ah hah, ah hah, ah hah.

4. He put Miss Mousie upon his knee, ah hah, ah hah (2 times)
   He put Miss Mousie on his knee, he said, "Missy Mouse will you marry me?"
   Ah hah, ah hah, ah hah.

5. "Without my Uncle Rat's consent," ah hah, ah hah (2 times)
   "Without my Uncle Rat's consent I wouldn't marry the president."
   Ah hah, ah hah, ah hah.

6. Where will the wedding supper be? ah hah, ah hah (2 times)
   Where will the wedding supper be? Way down yonder in a hollow tree.
   Ah hah, ah hah, ah hah.

7. What will the wedding supper be? ah hah, ah hah (2)
   What will the wedding supper be? Two green beans and a black-eyed pea.
   Ah hah, ah hah, ah hah.

8. They all went swimming across the lake, ah hah, ah hah (2 times)
   They all went swimming across the lake, they all got swallowed by a big black snake.
   Ah hah, ah hah, ah hah.

9. There's bread and cheese upon the shelf, ah hah, ah hah (2 times)
   There's bread and cheese upon the shelf, if you want any more you better get it yourself.
   Ah hah, ah hah, ah hah.

FROG IN THE SPRING

(Keemo Kymo)

Ukulele tuning: gCEA

Traditional

Chorus: hy, muh ho, a rick-y tick-y, tum-my tick-le, nip cat, sing song, king kong kit-ty won't you ky-me-o.

2. The frog could dance and he could sing,
   King kong kitty won't you ky-me-o,
   He made the woods around him ring,
   King kong kitty won't you ky-me-o.
   Chorus

3. Who's been here since I've been gone?
   King kong kitty won't you ky-me-o,
   A pretty little man with his new shoes on,
   King kong kitty won't you ky-me-o.
   Chorus

4. "A pretty little dandy man," said she,
   King kong kitty won't you ky-me-o,
   "With a crooked back and a striped knee,"
   King kong kitty won't you ky-me-o.
   Chorus

5. Mouse went swimming across the lake,
   King kong kitty won't you ky-me-o,
   He got swallowed by a big black snake,
   King kong kitty won't you ky-me-o.
   Chorus

Many versions of this song exist. This one was given to me by Lawrence Older
of Middle Grove, New York, near Mt. Pleasant in the southern Adirondacks.

GOOBER PEAS

A fabled staple of the Confederate army during the Civil War -- boiled peanuts!

Traditional

1.Sit-ting by the road-side on a sum-mer's day, chat-ting with my mess-mates, pass-ing time a-way,

ly-ing in the shad-ow un-der-neath the trees, good-ness how de-li - cious, eat-ing goo-ber peas.

Chorus: Peas, peas, peas, peas, eat-ing goo-ber peas, good-ness how de-li - cious, eat-ing goo-ber peas.

2. Just before the battle, the Gen'ral hears a row,
   He says, "The Yanks are coming, I hear their rifles now!"
   He turns around in wonder, and what do you think he sees?
   The Georgia Militia, eating goober peas!
   CHORUS

THE GRAND OLD DUKE OF YORK

Ukulele tuning: gCEA

Traditional

In Greek mythology Sisyphus, the evil king of Ephyra, was condemned to roll a giant boulder up to the top of a mountain only to have it roll back down once the top was reached. Over and over again this futile task was to be repeated for all eternity. Rather reminds one of the Grand Duke of York, don't you think?

HARRY TO THE FERRY

Ukulele tuning: gCEA

Traditional drinking song

HENRY THE EIGHTH

Ukulele tuning: gCEA

FRED MIURRAY & R.P. WESTON

The rock group Herman's Hermits from England soared this song to the top of the charts in 1965. It was a revival from the 1910 British music hall, the signature song of comic entertainer Harry Champion.

HAUL AWAY, JOE

Ukulele tuning: gCEA

Traditional

1.O when I was a lit - tle boy and so my moth - er told me,
2.Lou - ie was the King of France be - fore the Rev - o - lu - tion,

Way, haul a - way,_____ we'll haul a - way, Joe._____ That
Way, haul a - way,_____ we'll haul a - way, Joe._____ But

if I did not kiss the girls my lips they would grow mol - dy,
then he got his head cut off which spoil'd his con - sti - tu - tion,

Way, haul a - way,_____ we'll haul a - way, Joe._____
Way, haul a - way,_____ we'll haul a - way, Joe._____

2. Louie was the King of France afore the revolution,
    Way, haul away, we'll haul away, Joe.
  But then he got his head cut off which spoiled his constitution,
    Way, haul away, we'll haul away, Joe.

3. Once I had a German girl and she was fat and lazy, etc.
  Now I've got a yeller girl, she darn near drives me crazy, etc.

4. St. Patrick was a gentleman, he come from decent people, etc.
  He built a church in Dublin town, and on it put a steeple, etc.

5. Once I was in Ireland a-diggin' turf and praties, etc.
  Now I'm on a lime-juice ship hauling on the braces, etc.

"Haul Away, Joe" is one of a class of sea songs known as Slow-Drag chanteys. These songs typically are short, simple, and were applied to brief tasks of hauling. The pull on the rope in "Haul Away, Joe" came when the word "Joe" was sung or shouted.

1924

HULLABALOO BELAY

Ukulele tuning: gCEA

Traditional

2. A fresh young fellow named Shallo Brown, hullabaloo belay, hullabaloo below belay,
   He followed my mother all 'round the town, hullabaloo belay.

3. One day when father was on the crown, etc.
   My mother ran off with Shallo Brown, etc.

4. My father said to me, "Me, boy," etc.
   To which I quickly made reply, etc.

5. My father slowly pined away, etc.
   Because my mother came back the next day, etc.

I'D RATHER HAVE FINGERS THAN TOES

Ukulele tuning: gCEA

Words by GELETT BURGESS

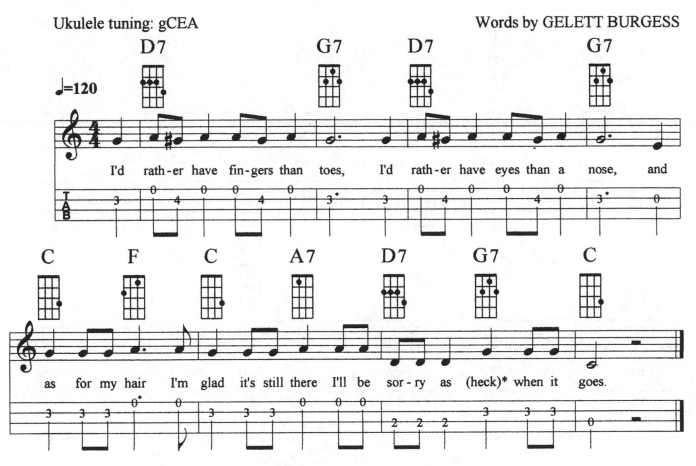

Lyrics under the music:

I'd rath-er have fin-gers than toes, I'd rath-er have eyes than a nose, and as for my hair I'm glad it's still there I'll be sor-ry as (heck)* when it goes.

* Or some other suitable word.

Gelett Burgess (1866-1951) was a popular American humorist known for his nonsensical verses. To the best of my knowledge there is no official melody for this verse. I turned it into a song when I was in college, and it proved a great favorite at sing-alongs, beer blasts, and beach parties. Burgess is perhaps better known for the following verse, and I leave it up to you to put it to music:

> I've never seen a purple cow,
> I never hope to see one;
> But I can tell you anyhow,
> I'd rather see than be one.

IT AIN'T GONNA RAIN NO MORE

Ukulele tuning: gCEA

Traditional

2. I never saw a purple cow, I never hope to see one,
   But I can tell you anyhow, I'd rather see than be one.*
   *A nonsense poem written in 1895 by Gelett Burgess.
   See also: "I'd Rather Have Fingers Than Toes."

3. What did the blackbird say to the crow, "It ain't gonna rain no mo,
   It ain't gonna hail, it ain't gonna snow, it ain't gonna rain no mo."

4. Peanut sitting on a railroad track, its heart was all a-flutter,
   Along came a choo-choo train, toot, toot, peanut butter.

Note: The melody of this song is very similar to "Father's Whiskers."

5. Mosquitoes they fly high, mosquitoes they fly low,
   If mosquitoes land on me they ain't gonna fly no mo.

6. Rich men ride in taxis, poor men ride a train,
   Bums they walk the rairoad tracks but they get there just the same.

7. When on a boat don't quarrel, you'll find without a doubt,
   A boat is not the proper place to have a falling out.

8. A boasting baby elephant said to the guinea pig,
   "I'm bigger when I'm little than you are when you're big."

I KNOW AN OLD LADY
WHO SWALLOWED A FLY

Ukulele tuning: gCEA

Traditional

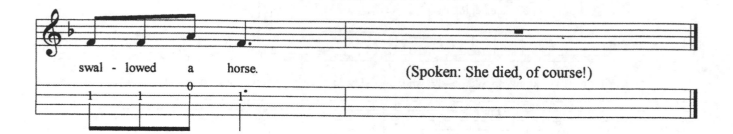

swal - lowed   a   horse.   (Spoken: She died, of course!)

1. I know an old lady who swallowed a fly,
   I don't know why she swallowed that fly,
   Maybe she'll die.

2. I know an old lady who swallowled a spider
   That wriggled and jiggled and tickled inside her.
   She swallowed the spider to catch the fly ... ETC.

3. I know an old lady who swallowed a bird,
   How absurd to swallow a bird.
   She swallowed the bird to catch the spider ... ETC.

4. I know an old lady who swallowed a cat,
   Fancy that, to swallow a cat.
   She swallowed the cat to catch the bird ... ETC.

5. I know an old lady who swallowed a dog,
   What a hog to swallow a dog.
   She swallowed the dog to catch the cat ... ETC.

6. I know an old lady who swallowed a goat,
   Right down her throat she swallowed the goat.
   She swallowed the goat to catch the dog ... ETC.

7. I know an old lady who swallowed a cow,
   I don't know how she swallowed that cow.
   She swallowed the cow to catch the goat ... ETC.

8. I know an old lady who swallowed a horse,
   She died, of course!

IT'S RAINING, IT'S POURING

Ukulele tuning: gCEA

Traditional

It's rain-ing, it's pour-ing, the old man is snor-ing, he went to bed and bumped his head and could-n't get up in the morn-ing.

Childhood memories for many of us recall sitting at a window on a soggy day wondering if the rain would ever stop so we could go out and play. How we would chant "Rain, rain, go away, come again some other day." There was hope in the saying that rain before seven clears by eleven. But woe betide us if it should rain on July 15, the feast of St. Swithun, for legend has it: *St. Swithun's Day, if thou dost rain, for forty days it will remain.*

IN CHINA THEY NEVER EAT CHILI

Ukulele tuning: gCEA

TRADITIONAL

The melody of the A part of this song is the familiar chorus of the Mexican folksong *Cielito Lindo*. Insert your favorite limerick in the B part. There are many to choose from on the Internet. Round and round the song goes, from A to B, then back again to A and a new limerick for B.

THE IRISH ROVER

Ukulele tuning: gCEA

Traditional

♩ = 120

In the year of our Lord, eigh-teen hun-dred and six, we set sail from the quay of Cork, we were

sail - ing a-way with a car - go of bricks for the grand Cit - y Hall in New York. We'd an

el - e - gant craft, it was rigged fore and aft, and how the trade winds drove her. She had

twen - ty - four masts and she stood sev - 'ral blasts, and we called her the I - rish Rov - er. We had

The Irish have a saying that the truth should never get in the way of a good story.

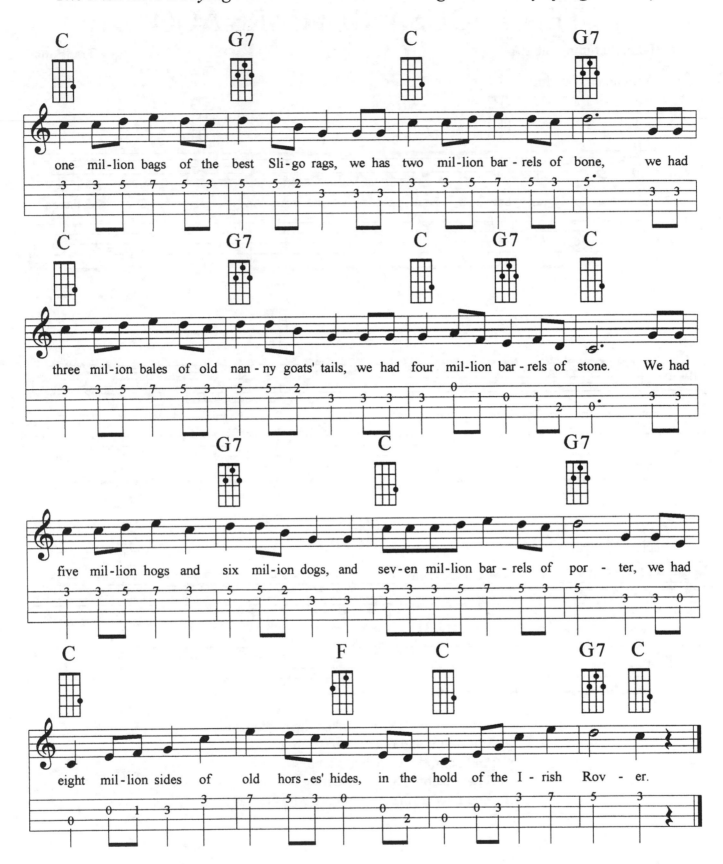

I WAS BORN ABOUT
TEN THOUSAND YEARS AGO

Ukulele tuning: gCEA

Tradtional

With an easy swing

I saw Satan when he looked the garden o'er,
SawAdam and Eve driven from the door.
And behind the bushes peeping,
Saw the apple they was eating,
And I swear that I'm the guy who ate the core.

I WAS BORN ABOUT TEN THOUSAND YEARS AGO

I saw Jonah when he shove off in the whale,
And I thought he'd never live to tell the tale.
But old Jonah'd eaten garlic,
And he gave the whale the colic,
So he coughed him up and let him outta jail.

A variation of this song is "The Man Who Rode The Mule Around the world."

I'm the man who rode the mule around the world,
I'm the man who rode the mule around the world,
I rode in Noah's ark, I'm as happy as a lark,
And I'll whup the man who says it isn't so.

I'm the man who rode the mule around the world, (2X)
I saw Moses on the water, I saw Pharoah and his daughter,
And I'll whup the man who says it isn't so.

I'm the man who rode the mule around the world, (2X)
I saw Pharoah's little kiddies, I built all the pyramiddies,
And I'll whup the man who says it isn't so.

Queen Elizabeth, she fell in love with me,
We were married in Milwaukee secretly,
But I rose up and I shook her, then ran off with Gen. Hooker
To shoot mosquitoes down in Tennessee.

I WISH I WAS SINGLE AGAIN

Ukulele tuning: gCEA

Traditional

I WISH I WAS SINGLE AGAIN

I married my wife, oh then, oh then,
I married my wife, oh then,
I married my wife she's the curse of my life,
And I wish I single again.

My wife she died, oh then, oh then,
My wife she died, oh then,
My wife she died and I laughted till I cried
To think I was single again.

I married another, oh then, oh then,
I married another, oh then,
I married another she's the devil's stepmother,
And I wish I was single again.

JOHN JACOB JINGLEHEIMER SCHMIDT

Ukulele tuning: gCEA

Traditional

This song is typically repeated over and over ad infinitum. Each time it's sung a little softer until finally, when patience is exhausted, it's bellowed out full volume.

ON TOP OF SPAGHETTI

To the tune of "On Top Of Old Smoky"

Ukulele tuning: gCEA

Traditional

2. It fell off the table and on to the floor,
   Then rolled down the hallway and right out the door.

3. It rolled to the garden and under a bush,
   And then my poor meatball was nothing but mush.

4. The mush was quite tasty, as tasty could be,
   And then the next summer, it grew into a tree.

5. The tree was all covered, all covered with moss,
   And on it grew meatballs with parnesan sauce.

6. So if you like s'ghetti, all covered with cheese,
   Hold on to the meatball whenever you sneeze.

JOHNNY WITH THE BANDY LEGS

Ukulele tuning: gCEA

Traditional

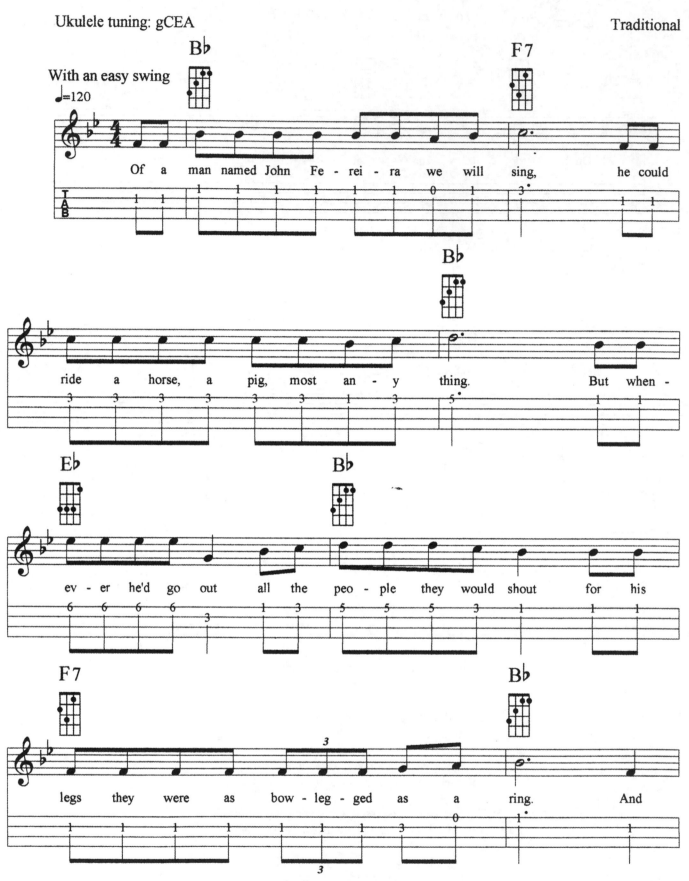

Of a man named John Fe - rei - ra we will sing, he could ride a horse, a pig, most an - y thing. But when - ev - er he'd go out all the peo - ple they would shout for his legs they were as bow - leg - ged as a ring. And

JOHNNY WITH THE BANDY LEGS

THE LILAC TREE
(PERSPICACITY)

Ukulele tuning: gCEA

GEORGE H. GARTLAN

A lit-tle boy and a lit-tle girl, in an ec-sta-cy of bliss, said the

lit-tle boy to the lit-tle girl, "Pray give me just one kiss." The

girl drew back in great sur-prise, "You're a strang-er, sir," said she, "And

I will give you just one kiss when the ap-ples grow on a li-lac tree!" The

LITTLE BROWN JUG

Ukulele tuning: gCEA

JOSEPH EASTBURN WINNER

1.My wife and I lived all a-lone in a lit-tle log hut we called our own;

she loved gin and I loved rum, I tell you what we'd lots of fun.

Chorus:

Ha, ha ha, you and me, Lit-tle Brown Jug don't I love thee!

Ha, ha, ha, you and me, Li-tle Brown Jug don't I love thee.

LITTLE BROWN JUG

2. When I go toiling to my farm,
   Little Brown Jug's tucked under my arm;
   I place it under a shady tree,
   Little Brown Jug 'tis you and me.
   CHO.

3. 'Tis you that makes me friends and foes,
   'Tis you that makes me wear old clothes,
   But seeing you so near my nose,
   Tip her up and down she goes.
   CHO.

4. If I'd a cow that gave such milk,
   I'd clothe her in the finest silk;
   I'd feed her on the choices hay
   And milk her forty times a day.
   CHO.

5. And when I die don't bury me at all,
   Just pickle my bones in alcohol,
   Put a bottle of booze at my head and feet
   And then I know that I will keep.
   CHO.

6. The rose is red, my nose is too,
   The violet's blue and so are you,
   And yet I guess before I stop
   We'd better take another drop.
   CHO.

LOLLY TOO DUM

Ukulele tuning: gCEA

Traditional

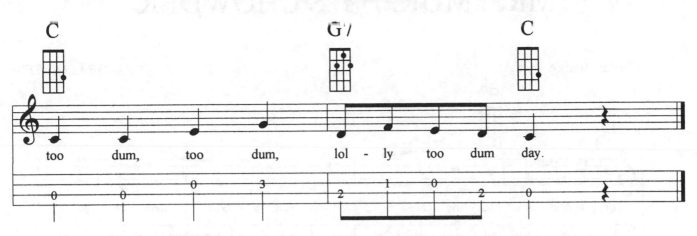

too   dum,   too   dum,   lol - ly   too   dum   day.

2. "You better go wash them dishes and hush that chattering tongue."
Lolly too dum, too dum, lolly too dum day.
"You better go wash them dishes and hush that chattering tongue.
You know that you want to get married and that you are too young."
Lolly too dum, too dum, lolly too dum day.

3. "Oh, pity my condition just as you would your own."
Lolly too dum, too dum, lolly too dum day.
"Oh, pity my condition just as you would your own.
For fourteen long years I've been living all alone."
Lolly too dum, too dum, lolly too dum day.

4. "Supposing I were willing, where would you get your man?"
Lolly too dum, too dum, lolly too dum day.
"Supposing I were willing, where would you get your man?"
"Lordy, mercy, Mama! I could marry that handsome Sam."
Lolly too dum, too dum, lolly too dum day.

5. "Supposing he should spite you like you done him before?"
Lolly too dum, too dum, lolly too dum day.
"Supposing he should spite you like you done him before?"
"Lordy, mercy, Mama! I could marry forty more."
Lolly too dum, too dum, lolly too dum day.

6. "There's peddler and there's tinkers and boys from the plow."
Lolly too dum, too dum, lolly too dum day.
"There's peddler and there's tinkers and boys from the plow.
Lordy, mercy, Mama! I'm a-gettin' that feelin' now."
Lolly too dum, too dum, lolly too dum day.

7. "Now my daughter's married and well for to do."
Lolly too dum, too dum, lolly too dum day.
"Now my daughter's married and well for to do.
Gather 'round young fellers, I'm in the market too."
Lolly too dum, too dum, lolly too dum day.

MRS. MURPHY'S CHOWDER

Ukulele tuning: gCEA

GEORGE L. GIEFER

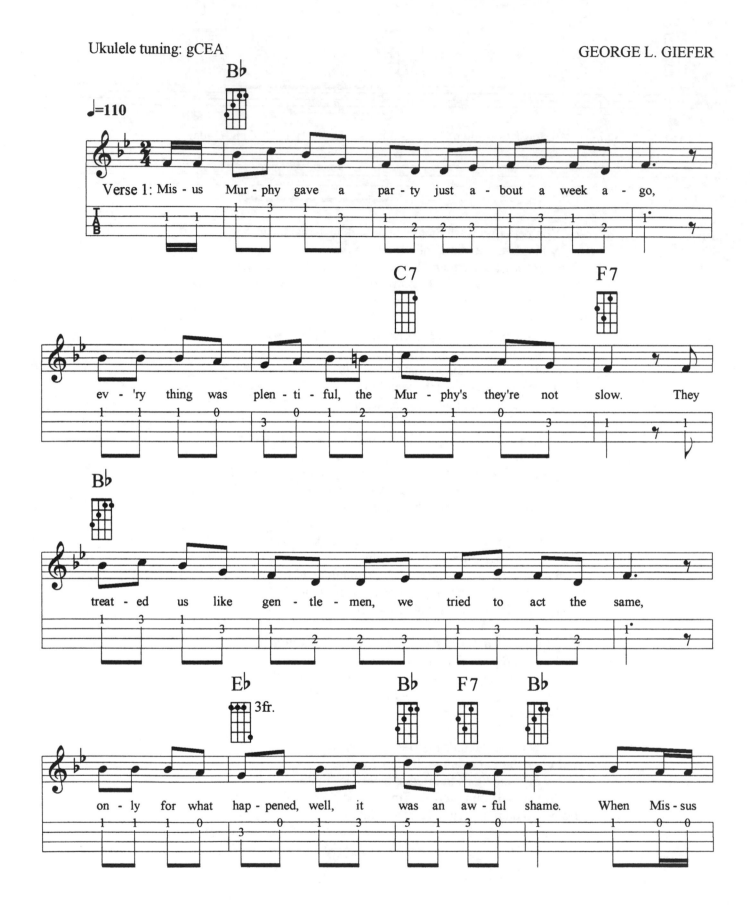

Verse 2: They dragged the pants from out the soup
And laid them on the floor.
Each man swore upon his life
He'd ne'er seen them before.
They were plastered up with mortar
And were worn out at the knee,
They had their many ups and down,
As we could plainly see.
And when Mrs. Murphy she came to,
She began to cry and pout;
She had them in the wash that day
And forgot to take them out.
Tim Nolan he excused himself
For what he said that night,
So we put music to the words
And sung with all out might:
Chorus

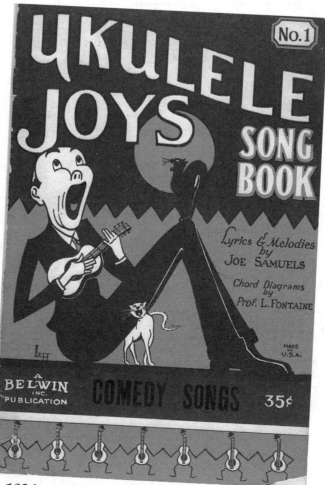

1926

MY GAL'S A CORKER
(SHE'S A NEW YORKER)

Ukulele tuning: gCEA

Traditional

MY GAL'S A CORKER

2. My gal's a corker, she's a New Yorker,
   I buy her ev'ry thing to keep her in style.
   She's got a pair of legs, just like two whisky kegs,
   Say, boys, that's where my money goes.

3. She's got a bulbous nose,
   Just like a big red rose...

4. She's got a head of hair,
   Just like a grizzly bear ...

5. She's got a pair of hips,
   Just like two battleships ...

6. She's got a pair of lips,
   Just like potato chips ...

7. She's got a pair of feet,
   Big as a Navy fleet ...

This song means no offense to the ladies. Many of the characteristics described could easily apply to the menfolk just as well, and there are probably a lot more that could be listed. Indeed, it's all in fun. But be careful, take heed: "There's many a true word spoken in jest."

OH! SUSANNA

Ukulele tuning: gCEA

STEPHEN C. FOSTER

I once was asked, "What's the name of that song they always play in the Old West movies, the one in the saloon scenes where there's a piano player wearing a striped shirt, arm garters, and a derby hat with a sign on the wall saying DON'T SHOOT THE PIANO PLAYER. "*Golden Slippers*," I suggested. "No, no, not that one!" came the emphatic response. I tried again, "How about *Turkey In The Straw?*" Again no luck. Then it dawned on me, "*Oh! Susanna?*" I asked. That time I struck paydirt, and it's no wonder. *Oh! Susanna* is one of America's best known songs and surely one of Foster's most popular.

Written in 1848, just at the time when the California Gold Rush was gaining momentum, the song became the unofficial anthem of prospecting "Forty-Niners" who came from Alabama and elsewhere with a "washpan" on their knee instead of a banjo. The song was written as a minstrel number with a lively polka beat that was popular at the time. Over 100,000 copies were eventually sold but allegedly Foster only received payment of $100. Because of uncertain copyright laws, many unscrupulous publishers printed the song without paying royalties.

OH, YOU CAN'T GET TO HEAVEN

Ukulele tuning: gCEA

Traditional

92

Oh, you can't get to heaven in a rocking chair,
'Cause the Lord don't want no lazybones there.
Oh, you can't get to heaven in a rocking chair,
'Cause the Lord don't want no lazybones there.

Oh, you can't get to heaven in a Chevrolet,
'Cause a Chevrolet don't go that way. ETC.

Oh, you can't get to heaven in a motor car,
'Cause a motor car don't go that far. ETC.

Oh, you can't get to heaven in a limousine,
'Cause the Lord don't have no gasoline. ETC.

Now if you get to heaven before I do,
Just drill a hole and pull me through. ETC.

Cliff Edwards, aka "Ukulele Ike," promoting his Columbia recording of "Singing in the Rain." He was the voice of Jiminy Cricket in the Walt Disney movie "Pinocchio" and sang "When You Wish Upon A Star" from the same movie.

OLD DAN TUCKER

Ukulele tuning: gCEA

Traditional

OLD DAN TUCKER

Verse 2. Old Dan Tucker came to town,
Riding a billy goat, leading a hound.
The hound he barked and the billy goat jumped,
Throw'd Dan Tucker a-straddle of a stump.
Chorus

Verse 3. Old Dan Tucker is a fine old man,
Washed his face in a frying pan,
Combed his hair with a wagon wheel,
Died with a toothache in his heel.
Chorus

Verse 4. Old Dan Tucker, he got drunk,
Fell in the fire and kicked out a chunk,
Got a live coal in his shoe,
Holy golamighty, how the ashes flew!
Chorus

Verse 5. Old Dan Tucker comes to town,
Swings the ladies round and round,
Swings one east and swings one west,
Swings with the one that he loves best.

I've Been Floating Down
THE OLD GREEN RIVER

Ukulele tuning: gCEA

BERT KALMER

JOE COOPER

THE OLD GREEN RIVER

Husbands out on the town who come staggering home in the wee hours
can certainly tell their wives some whoppers, but this one tops them all!

PEEPING THRU THE KNOTHOLE
ON GRANDPA'S WOODEN LEG

Ukulele tuning: gCEA

Traditional

2. While peeping thru the knothole
   Of Grandpa's wooden leg,
   Who put the shore so near the ocean?
   Who cut the sleeves
   Out of dear old daddy's vest,
   And dug up Fido's bones to build a sewer?

3. While walking in the moonlight,
   The bright and sunny moonlight,
   She kissed me in the eye with a tomato.
   A snake's belt slips
   Because he has no hips,
   So he wears his necktie around his middle.

4. I fell from a window,
   A second story window,
   And caught my eyebrow on the window sill.
   Go fetch the Listerine,
   Sister's got a beau,
   And Grandma's teeth will soon fit the baby.

George Formby, "The Ukulele Man." British music hall comic entertainer and virtuoso banjo-ukulele player.

THE PIG SONG

Ukulele tuning: gCEA

Traditional

It was back in late Sep - tem - ber,_____ how
As I lay there in the gut - ter _____ my

well I do re - mem - ber,_____ I was
heart was all a - flut - ter,_____ and a

walk - ing down the street in drunk - en pride._____ When my
la - dy pass - ing by was heard to say,_____ "You can

knees be - gan to stut - ter,_____ I fell down in the gut - ter,_____ and a
tell a man who booz - es _____ by the com - pan - y he choos - es,"_____ and with

F   C7

pig   came   up   and   lay   down   by   my   side.
that   the   up   pig   got   up   and   walked   a - way.

POLLY WOLLY DOODLE

Ukulele tuning: gCEA

Traditional

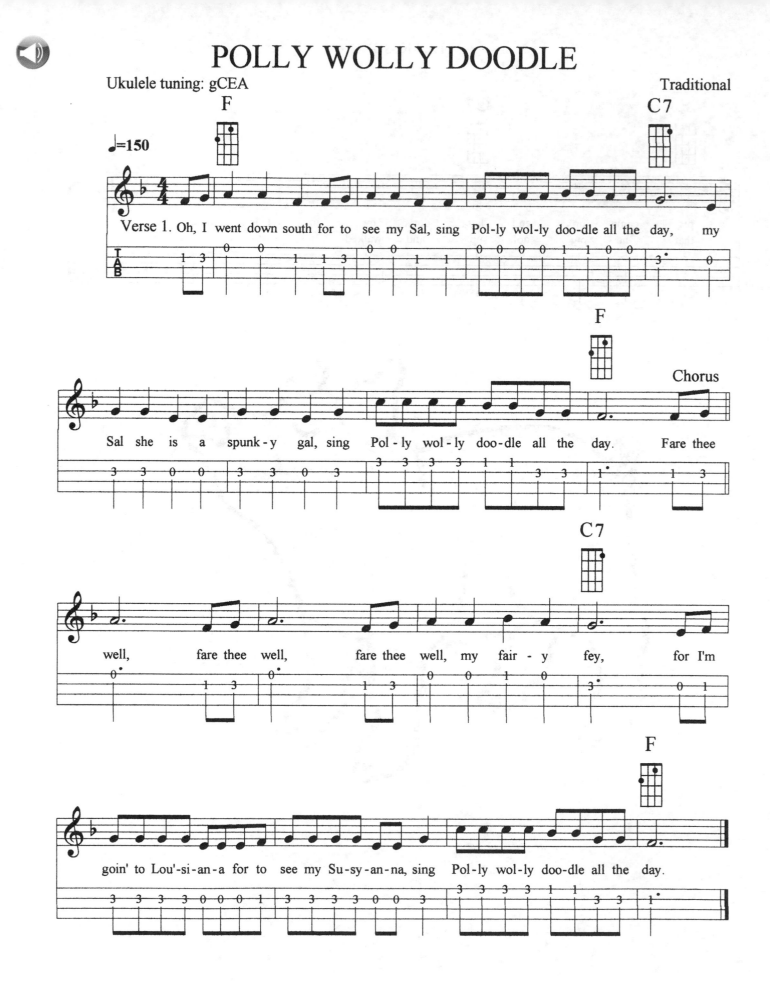

POLLY WOLLY DOODLE

Verse 2. Grasshopper sitting on a railroad track,
Sing Polly wolly doodle all the day,
A-pickin' his teeth with a carpet tack,
Sing Polly wolly doodle all the day.
Chorus:
   Fare thee well, fare thee well,
   Fare thee well, my fairy fey,
   For I'm goin' to Lou'siana
   For to see my Susyanna,
   Sing Polly wolly doodle all the day.

Verse 3. My gal she is a maiden fair,
Sing Polly wolly doodle all the day,
With curly eyes and laughing hair,
Sing Polly wolly doodle all the day.
Chorus

Verse 4. Behind the barn down on my knees,
Sing Polly wolly doodle all the day,
I thought I heard a chicken sneeze,
Sing Polly wolly doodle all the day.
Chorus

Verse 5. Sneezed so hard with the whooping cough,
Sing Polly wolly doodle all the day,
Sneezed its head and tail right off,
Sing Polly wolly doodle all the day.
Chorus

THE QUARTERMASTER'S SONG

Ukulele tuning: gCEA

Traditional

1.For it's BEER, beer, beer that makes you want to cheer in the Corps, in the Corps, for it's

beer, beer, beer that makes you want to cheer in the Quar-ter-mas-ter's, Quar-ter-mas-ter's Corp. My

CHORUS

eyes grow dim, I can - not see, I

have HEY! not HO! brought my specs with me.

2. For it's WHISKEY, whiskey, whiskey,
   That makes you feel so frisky, etc.
   CHO.

3. For it's BRANDY, brandy, brandy,
   That makes you feel just dandy, etc.
   CHO.

4. For it's WATER, water, water,
   That mkes you feel you oughter, etc.
   CHO.

5. For it's WINE, wine, wine,
   That makes you feel so fine, etc.
   CHO.

6. For it's ALE, ale, ale,
   That makes you grow so pale, etc.
   CHO.

7. For it's RYE, rye, rye,
   That makes you feel so spry, etc.
   CHO.

8. For it's RUM, rum, rum
   Puts your stomach on the bum, etc.
   CHO.

9. For it's SHERRY, sherry, sherry,
   That makes you feel so merry, etc.
   CHO.

10. For it's VERMOUTH, vermouth, vermouth,
    That makes you feel uncouth, etc.
    CHO

Now make up your own verses for PORT, TEA, GIN, TEQUILLA, BOURBON, etc.

SHE'LL BE COMING 'ROUND THE MOUNTAIN

Ukulele tuning: gCEA

A Parody

Traditional

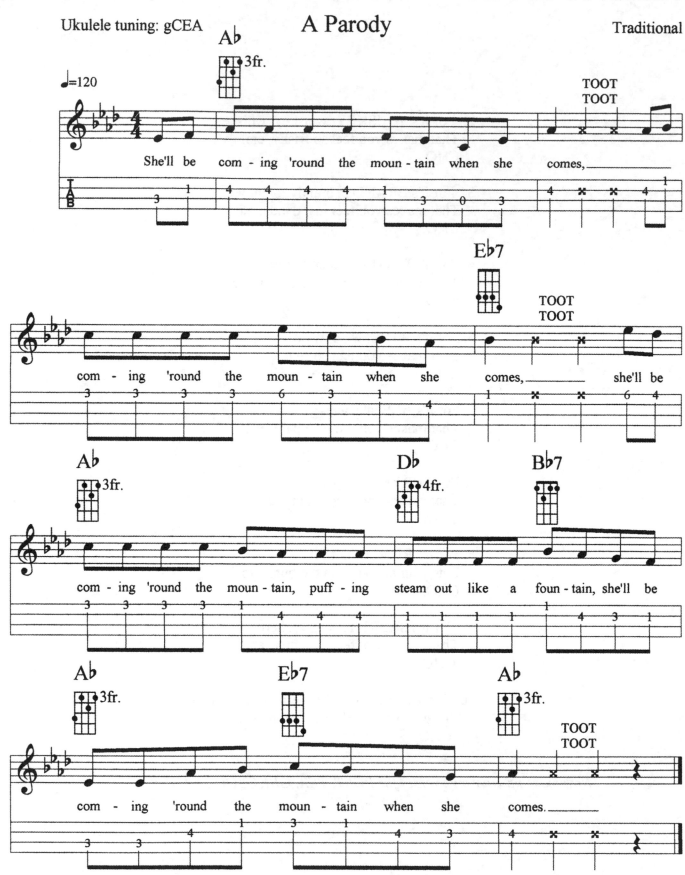

She'll be riding six white horses when she comes (WHOA, HORSE!), etc.

She'll be wearing pink pajamas when she comes (WHISTLE, WHISTLE), etc.

We'll all go out to meet her when she comes (HI! BABE!), etc.

We'll kill the old red rooster when she comes (COCK-A-DOODLE -DOO), etc.
(We'll kill the old red rooster, he ain't crowing like he useter) etc.

We'll all have chicken dumplings when she comes (CLUCK, CLUCK), etc.

THE SOW TOOK THE MEASLES

Ukulele tuning: gCEA

Traditional

2. What do you think I did with her hide?
Made the best saddle you ever did ride.
Sadle or bridle or some such thing,
The sow took the measles and died in the spring.

3. What do you think I did with her tail?
Made the best whip you ever did flail.
Whip or flail handle or some such thing,
The sow took the measles and died in the spring.

4. What do you think I did with her hair?
Made the best satin you ever did wear.
Satin or silk or some such thing,
The sow took the measles and died in the spring.

5. What do you think I did with her feet?
Made the best pickles you ever did eat.
Pickles or glue or some such thing,
The sow took the measles and died in the spring.

The whimsical whoppers in this song certainly stretch the imagination.
They're reminiscent of those in the "Derby Ram" found elsewhere in this book.

THERE AIN'T NO FLIES ON ME

Ukulele tuning: gCEA

Traditional

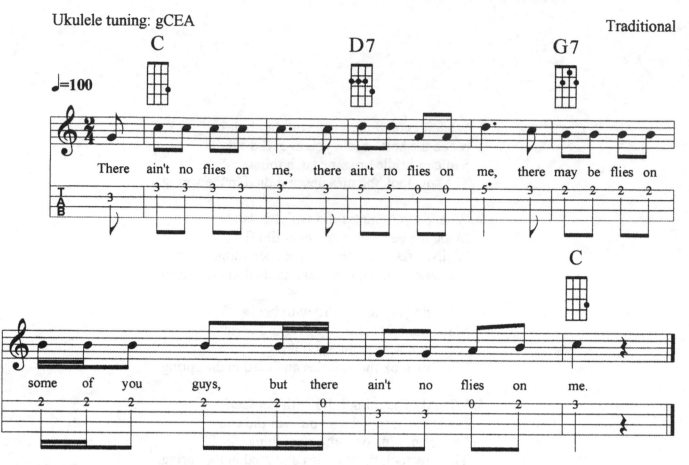

There ain't no flies on me, there ain't no flies on me, there may be flies on some of you guys, but there ain't no flies on me.

There ain't no bugs on me,
There ain't no bugs on me,
There may be bugs on some of you mugs, but
There ain't no bugs on me.

Little bugs have little-er bugs
Upon their back to bite 'em,
Little-er bugs have little-er bugs
And so on ad infinitum.

Some folks say that fleas are black
But I know that it ain't so,
'Cause Mary had a little lamb
Whose fleas was white as snow.

There was a cat down on the farm,
She ate a ball of yarn,
When her kittens came along
They all had sweaters on.

Skeeters they fly high,
Skeeters they fly low,
If any skeeter lands on me.
It ain't gonna fly no mo'.

Does the melody sound familiar? It's almost the same as that for "Father's Whiskers."

110

THREE BLIND MICE

Ukulele tuning: gCEA

Traditional

THREE JOLLY FISHERMEN

Ukulele tuning: gCEA

Traditional

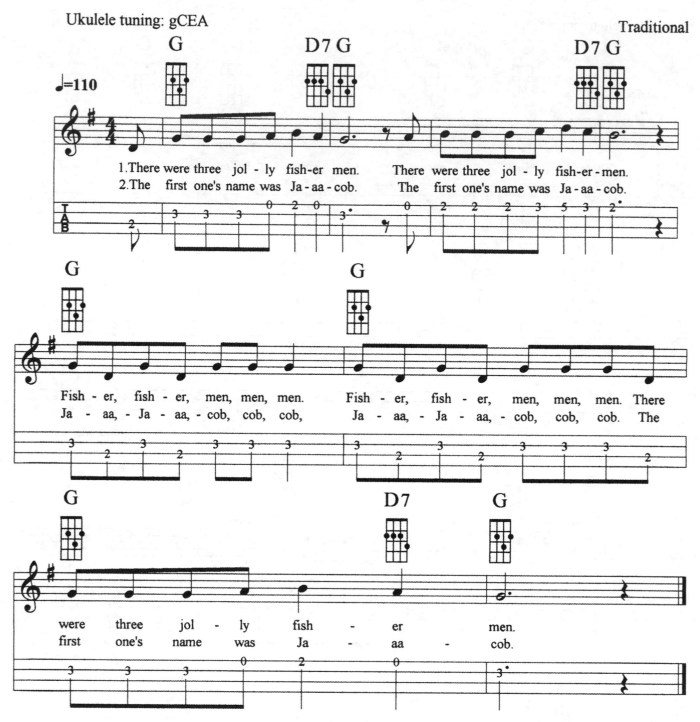

3. The second one's name was Isaac.
   The second one's name was Isaac.
   I-I- zic, zic, zic.
   I-I-zic, zic, zic.
   The second one's name was I-saac.

THREE JOLLY FISHERMEN

4. The third one's name was Abraham.
   The third one's name was Abraham.
   Abra, Abra, ham, ham, ham.
   Abra, Abra, ham, ham, ham.
   The third one's name was Abraham.

5. They all went down to Jerico.
   They all went down to Jerico.
   Jeri, Jeri, co, co, co.
   Jeri, Jeri, co, co, co.
   They all went down to Jerico.

6. They should have gone to Amster-sssh!.
   They should have gone to Amster-sssh!
   Amster, Amster, sssh! sssh! sssh!
   Amster, Amster, sssh! sssh! sssh!
   They should have gone to Amster-sssh!

7. I must not say that naughty word.
   I must not say that naughty word.
   Naughty, naughty, word, word, word.
   Naughty, naughty, word, word, word.
   I must not say that naughty word.

8. I think I'll say it anyway.
   I think I'll say it anyway.
   Any, any, way, way, way.
   Any, any, way, way, way.
   I think I'll say it anyway.

9. They should have gone to Amsterdam.
   They should have gone to Amsterdam.
   Amster, Amster, dam, dam, dam.
   Amster, Amster, dam, dam, dam.
   They should have gone to Amsterdam.

THROW IT OUT THE WINDOW

(To the tune of *Polly Wolly Doodle*)

Ukulele tuning: gCEA

Traditional

THROW IT OUT THE WINDOW

Now try substituting your favorite nursery rhymes

Mary had a little lamb, its fleece was white as snow,
And ev'rywhere that Mary went, she threw it out the window.
The window, the window,
And ev'rywhere that Mary went, she threw it out the window.

Little Jack Horner sat in a corner eating a Christmas pie,
He stuck in hs thumb and pulled out a plum,
And threw it out the window. Etc.

Hickory, dickory dock. The mouse ran up the clock.
The clock struck one, and done he run,
And they threw him out the window. Etc.

Tom, Tom, the piper's son, stole a pig and away he run.
The pig was eat, and Tom was beat,
And they threw him out the window. Etc.

Little Miss Moffett, sat on a tuffet, eating her curds and whey,
Along came a spider and sat down beside her
And she threw it out the window. Etc.

Jack and Jill went up the hill to fetch a pail of water,
Jack fell down and broke his crown
And Jill threw him out the window. Etc.

Humpty Dumpty sat on a wall, Humpty Dumpty had a great fall.
All the king's horses and all the king's men
Threw him out the window. Etc.

Hey, diddle, diddle, the cat and the fiddle, the cow jumped over the moon,
The lttle dog laughed to see such sport.
And they threw him out the window. Etc.

Etc.
(Groan ...)

TURKEY IN THE STRAW

Ukulele tuning: gCEA

TRADITIONAL

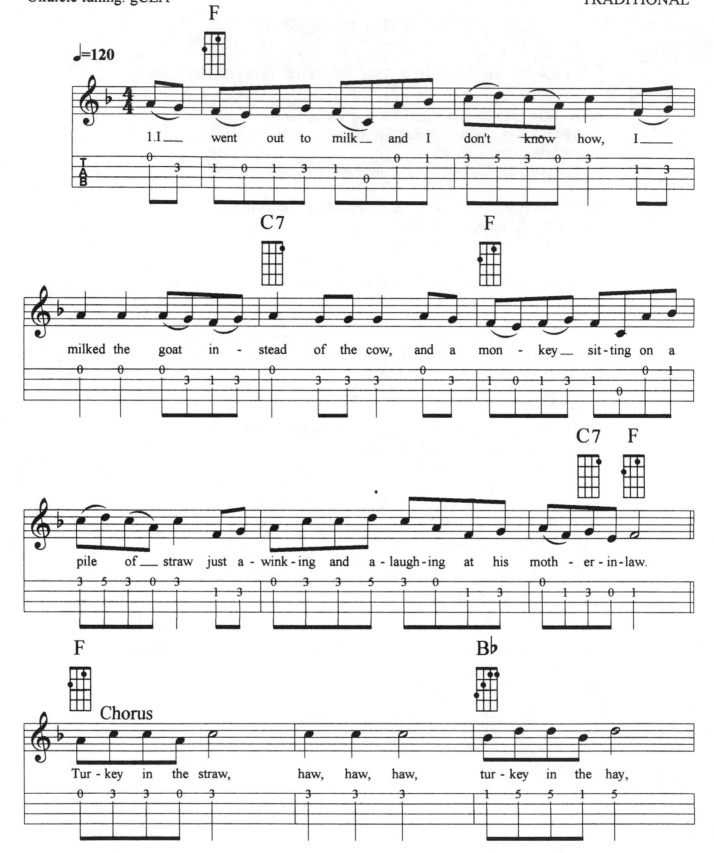

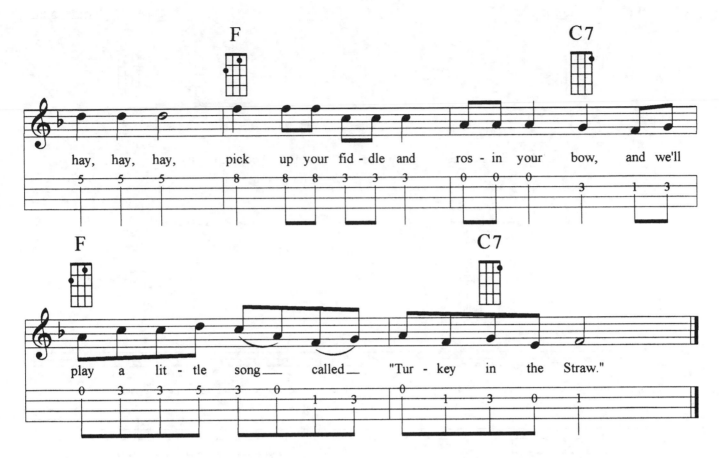

hay, hay, hay, pick up your fid - dle and ros - in your bow, and we'll

play a lit - tle song called "Tur - key in the Straw."

2. Well, if frogs had wings and snakes had hair,
And automobiles went fying through the air,
And if watermellons grew on a huckleberry vine,
We'd still have winter in the summertime.
Chorus

3. I had an old hen and she had a wooden leg,
Just the best old hen that ever laid an egg.
She laid more eggs than any on the farm,
And another little drink won't do us any harm.
Chorus

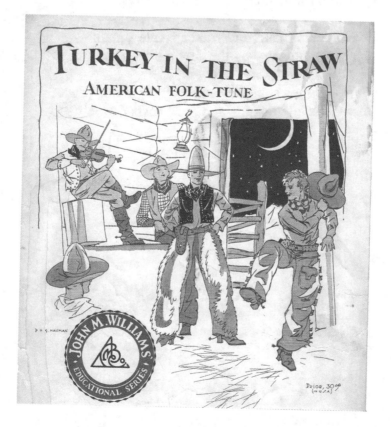

WHISTLE, DAUGHTER, WHISTLE

Ukulele tuning: gCEA

Traditional

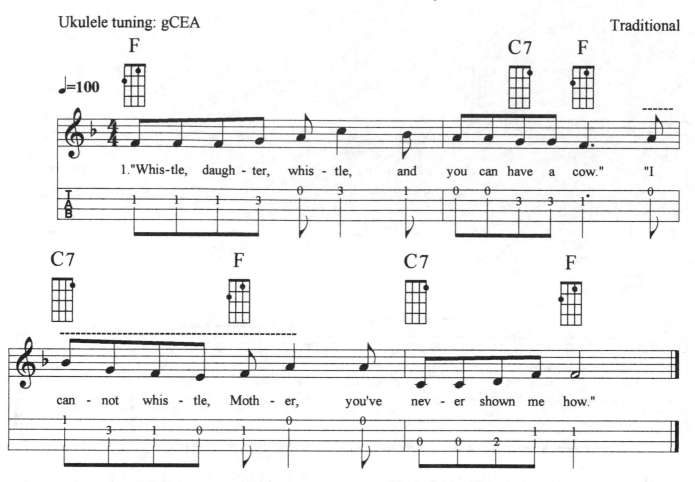

2. "Whistle, daughter, whistle, and you can have a horse."
"I've never whistled in my life, I cannot now, of course."

3. "Whistle, daughter, whistle, and you can have a sheep."
"I cannot whistle, Mother, and neither can I sleep."

4. "Whistle, daughter, whistle, and you can have a man."
(Whistle the notes indicated by the dotted lines, then sing) "I'll do the best I can."

5. "And now my daughter's married and well for to do.
So learn to whistle all you girls and get a husband too."

YANKEE DOODLE

Ukulele tuning: gCEA

Traditional

Although the origin of the word "Yankee" is obscure, it is thought that "Doodle" comes from the German word for a simpleton. The word "macaroni" refers not to pasta but to a foppish affectation like the term "dandy." Thus, poor Yankee Doodle is depicted as something of a silly, comical, foolish fellow.

THE WREN SONG

Ukulele tuning: gCEA

Tradtional Irish

1.The wren, the wren, the king of all birds, St. Ste-phen's Day was caught in the furze, al-

though he was lit-tle his hon-or was great, jump up, me lads, and give him a treat.

CHORUS

Up with the ket-tle and down with the pan, and give us a pen-ny to bur-y the wren.

The hunting of the wren is a traditional festivity celebrated in Ireland on the day after Christmas, December 26, St. Stephen's Day. An artificial bird is often hidden in the bushes and search parties go looking for it with much clamor and fanfare. Paraders and bands of musicians walk through the streets with blackened faces or wearing masks and disguises, often dressed in costumes, particularly those made of straw. The searchers are known variously as mummers, straw boys, or wren boys. Part of the ritual is begging for money, the proceeds from which can underwrite a gathering at the local pub, an evening dance, or some community charity like schools or churches. Another form of celebration is to mount the discovered wren on a pole decorated with a wreath of ribbons and flowers, which would then be surrounded by musicians, dancers, and merrymakers. There are many variants of the song, but all exaggerate the trial of the hunt, carrying the bird home, serving it up for a dinner feast, or using the collected funds for the bird's burial.

2. We followed the wren three miles or more,
   Three miles or more, three miles or more,
   Through hedges and ditches and heaps of snow
   At six o'clock in the morning.

3. Rolly, Rolley, where is your nest?
   It's in the bush that I love best,
   It's in the bush, the holly tree,
   Where all the boys do follow me.

4. As I went out to hunt and all,
   I met a wren upom the wall,
   Up with me wattle and gave him a fall,
   And brought him here to show you all.

5. A little box is under my arm,
   A tuppence or penny will do it no harm,
   For we are the boys who came your way
   To bring in the wren on St Stephen's Day.

Here's another version sung to a different melody and sometimes called "The Cutty Wren" or "Hunting The Wren."

"We'll hunt the wren," says Robbin to Bobbin,
"We'll hunt the wren," says Richard to Robin,
"We'll hunt the wren," says Jack o'the land,
"We'll hunt the wren," says everyone.

"Where, oh where?" says Robbin to Bobbin,
"Where, oh where?" says Richard to Robin,
"Where, oh where?" says Jack o'the land,
"Where, oh where?" says everyone ... "In Yonder green bush" ...

"How get him down?" ... "With sticks and stones" ...

"How get him home?" ... "The brewers big cart" ...

"How will we cook him? ... "In bloody great cauldrons" ...

"How will we eat him?" ... "With hatchets and cleavers, " ...

"Who'll come to dinner? ... "The king and the queen" ...

"Eyes to the blind," says Robin to Bobbin,
" Legs to the lame," says Richard to Robin,
" Luck to the poor,"says Jack o'the land,
" And bones to the dogs," says everyone.

More Great Books from Dick Sheridan...

CELTIC SONGS FOR THE TENOR BANJO
37 Traditional Songs and Instrumentals
by Dick Sheridan

INCLUDES TAB

Jigs & reels, hornpipes, airs, dances and more are showcased in this exciting 37 collection drawn from Ireland, Scotland, Wales, Cornwall, Brittany and the Isle of Man. Each traditional song – with its lilting melody and rich accompaniment harmony – has been carefully selected and presented for tenor banjo in both note form and tablature with chord symbols and diagrams. Lyrics and extra verses are included for many songs. Includes: All Through The Night, Blackbird Will You Go, The Campbells Are Coming, Garry Owen, Harvest Home, O'Gallaher's Frolics, Saddle The Pony, Swallow Tail Jig and many more.
00122477..$14.99

LOVE SONGS FOR UKULELE
37 Love Songs in All
by Dick Sheridan

INCLUDES TAB

Romance is in the air, and here to prove it are 37 of the best and most enduring love songs ever! Here are romantic treasures from the musical theater; whimsical novelty numbers; ballads of both true and false love; songs for sweethearts, lovers and hopefuls; sad songs of longing and heartbreak; and barbershop favorites. The creative ukulele arrangements in notes, tab & chords make each song rewarding and fun to play. Includes: Beautiful Dreamer • Careless Love • I Love You Truly • Let Me Call You Sweetheart • My Gal Sal • Avalon • Frankie and Johnny • Secrets • Margie • Oh By Jingo! • I Want a Girl • Ida • Moonlight Bay • and many more. Arranged in standard C tuning for soprano, concert and tenor ukuleles, with tunes readily adaptable to baritone ukulele, tenor guitars, and guitar-tuned banjos.
00119342..$12.99

HALLELUJAH UKULELE
19 of the Best and Most Beloved Hymns & Spirituals
by Dick Sheridan

INCLUDES TAB

Here's a truly special collection of gospel favorites drawn from the traditions of many faiths and cultures. It brings a delightful mix of treasured worship songs, including: Amazing Grace • Go Down, Moses • Hine Mah Tev • In the Garden • The Old Rugged Cross • Rock My Soul • Swing Low, Sweet Chariot • What a Friend We Have in Jesus • and many more. This book contains basic melodies with notes and tablature, exciting creative harmonies, chord symbols and large, easy-to-read diagrams, and selected solos and lyrics.
00122113..$12.99

YULETIDE FAVORITES FOR UKULELE
A Treasury of Christmas Hymns, Carols & Songs
by Dick Sheridan

INCLUDES TAB

This holiday collection for uke features easy-to-read arrangements with melody in standard notation, tablature, lyrics, chord symbols and diagrams. Selections include traditional American and English carols as well as songs from other countries. Seasonal and holiday tunes are featured, as well as wassails, ancient airs and dances.
00109749..$9.99

IRISH SONGS FOR UKULELE
by Dick Sheridan

INCLUDES TAB

Shamrocks, shillelaghs and shenanigans…they are all here in this collection of 55 fabulous Irish favorites! Each song is specifically arranged for the ukulele, with the melody in both standard notation and easy-to-read tab. Includes: An Irish Lullaby • The Band Played On • Cockles and Mussels • Danny Boy • The Irish Rover • McNamara's Band • Peg O' My Heart • The Rose of Tralee • and dozens more.
00103153..$15.99

COLLEGE FIGHT SONGS & ALMA MATERS FOR UKULELE
by Dick Sheridan

INCLUDES TAB

For the varsity football enthusiast, as well as for the perennial college sophomore, here are over 40 of the best-known team songs from major conferneces all across the country in easy-to-play arrangements for the ever-popular ukulele. Even if your own school connection is not included, you'll recognize many of these songs made popular through sporting events, radio and TV broadcasts. Includes arrangements in standard notation and tablature, with lyrics and melodies.
00124458..$15.99

SONGS OF THE CIVIL WAR FOR UKULELE
by Dick Sheridan

INCLUDES TAB

25 tunes of the era that boosted morale, championed causes, pulled on the heartstrings, or gave impetus to battle. Includes: All Quiet Along the Potomac, Aura Lee, Battle Hymn of the Republic, Dixie, The Girl I Left Behind Me, John Brown's Body, When Johnny Comes Marching Home and more - all in standard C tuning, with notation, tablature and accompanying lyrics. The book also includes notes on the songs, historical commentary, and a handy chord chart!
00001588..$14.99

P.O. Box 17878 - Anaheim Hills, CA 92817
(714) 779-9390   www.centerstream-usa.com

More Great Ukulele Books from Centerstream...

CHRISTMAS UKULELE, HAWAIIAN STYLE

Play your favorite Christmas songs Hawaiian style with expert uke player Chika Nagata. This book/CD pack includes 12 songs, each played 3 times: the first and third time with the melody, the second time without the melody so you can play or sing along with the rhythm-only track. Songs include: Mele Kalikimaka (Merry Christmas to You) • We Wish You a Merry Christmas • Jingle Bells (with Hawaiian lyrics) • Angels We Have Heard on High • Away in a Manger • Deck the Halls • Hark! The Herald Angels Sing • Joy to the World • O Come, All Ye Faithful • Silent Night • Up on the Housetop • We Three Kings.
00000472 Book/CD Pack $19.95

FUN SONGS FOR UKULELE

INCLUDES TAB

50 terrific songs in standard notation and tablature for beginning to advanced ukulele players. Includes Hawaiian songs, popular standards, classic Western, Stephen Foster and more, with songs such as: The Darktown Strutters Ball • I'm Always Chasing Rainbows • Hot Lips • Gentle Annie • Maikai Waipio • Whispering • Ja-Da • China Boy • Colorado Trail • and many more. Also includes a chord chart and a special section on how to hold the ukulele.
00000407.. $14.95

ULTIMATE LIT'L UKULELE CHORDS, PLUS

INCLUDES TAB

by Kahuna Uke (aka Ron Middlebrook)
This handy 6' x 9' guide in the popular C tuning provides all the ukulele chords you'll ever need or use. The diagrams are easy to use and follow, with all the principal chords in major and minor keys, in all the different chords positions. Plus, there are sections on How to Begin, Scales on All Strings, Note Studies, and Chord Modulations (great to use for intros & endings!). This handy 32 page guide fits right in a case perfectly. Happy strumming, you'll Mahalo me latter.
00001351.. $7.99

ASAP UKULELE

INCLUDES TAB

Learn How to Play the Ukulele Way
by Ron Middlebrook
This easy new method will teach you the ukulele ASAP! Each exercise in the book has been designed to teach you the most popular key chord combinations and patterns that you'll see in hundreds of songs. The tunes taught here include: Auld Lang Syne - My Bonnie Lies Over the Ocean - Oh! Susanna - Peg of My Heart - Red River Valley - Tiger Rag - and many more. You can strum the chords for each, or play the easy-to-follow melody.
00001359.. $14.99

KEV'S QUICKSTART FINGERSTYLE UKULELE

INCLUDES TAB

by Kevin Rones
Go Beyond Three Chords And A Strum!
This book/CD package is for anyone who want to become better at playing the ukulele.
Newbies: Have fun learning how to play Fingerstyle Ukulele quickly without having to read music! **Ukulele Strummers:** Tired of strumming the same old chords? This book will have you picking in no time! **Indie Artist and Songwriters:** Expand you song writing and performance with Fingerstyle Ukulele. **Guitars players:** If you already play guitar this book is your shortcut into learning Ukulele. Learn arrangements written specifically for Fingerstyle Ukulele: Bach, Blues, Folk, Celtic and more!
000001590.. $17.99

UKULELE FOR COWBOYS

INCLUDES TAB

40 of your favorite cowboy songs in chords, standard notation and tab. Includes: Buffalo Gals • Night Herding Song • Doney Gal • Old Chisholm Trail • The Big Corral • Ragtime Cowboy Joe • Colorado Trail • Old Paint • Yellow Rose of Texas • Green Grow the Lilacs • and many more. Also includes a chord chart, historical background on many of the songs, and a short story on the history of the Hawaiian Cowboy.
00000408.. $14.99

UKULELE SONGBOOK

INCLUDES TAB

compiled by Ron Middlebrook
This terrific collection for beginning to advanced ukulele players features easy arrangements of 50 great songs, in standard notation and tablature. Also teaches popular strum patterns, and how to tune the uke.
00000248.. $9.95

UKULELE CHORDS

Plus Intros and Endings
by Ron Middlebrook
This handy chart includes clear, easy-to-see chord fingerings in all keys, plus a bonus section that provides favorite intros and endings in different keys. Also includes information on relative tuning.
00000246.. $2.95

SONGS OF THE CIVIL WAR FOR UKULELE

by Dick Sheridan
25 tunes of the era that boosted morale, championed causes, pulled on the heartstrings, or gave impetus to battle. Includes: All Quiet Along the Potomac, Aura Lee, Battle Hymn of the Republic, Dixie, The Girl I Left Behind Me, John Brown's Body, When Johnny Comes Marching Home and more - all in standard C tuning, with notation, tablature and accompanying lyrics. The book also includes notes on the songs, historical commentary, and a handy chord chart!
00001588.. $14.99

THE LOW G STRING TUNING UKULELE

INCLUDES TAB

by Ron Middlebrook
25 popular songs for the ukulele in standard music notation, tablature and easy chords. To get the most out of this book, you'll want to replace the fourth (high G) string with one of a heavier gauge and tune it an octave lower to get that full, deep sound – a lá Hawaiian uke virtuoso Jesse Kalima – in playing the melodies in this book. The chords can be played with or without the low G sound.
00001534 Book/CD Pack $19.99

P.O. Box 17878 - Anaheim Hills, CA 92817
(714) 779-9390   www.centerstream-usa.com

Those using
Centerstream
Books & DVDs

The Competition